The Thoroughbred Horse: Origin, Distribution, Breeding, Conformation, Uses

J. A. Estes

HISTORY: How a Change in the Technique of Battle Changed the Shape of Horses; Origins of the Breed; Early Records; Establishment of the Closed Registry.

MANY histories of the Thoroughbred entrap themselves somewhat by beginning simply with the horse. The present pages, in the endeavor to account for the Thoroughbred only, will skip lightly over all that goes before the year 1700, since the history of this breed, as we know it, begins at about that time. That there were horses in England at the beginning of the English history is well known; that there has been racing wherever there were horses goes without saying, the nature of man being what it is.

The historical background necessary is the observation that the shift from the heavy horse to the light horse became a necessity as medieval warfare became modern. When the fighting unit was a mounted knight in full armor, a horse capable of bearing a burden which sometimes must have amounted to 450 pounds was the desirable type. When the massed chivalry of France,

Background of War at Agincourt and Crecy and Poitiers, went down in bloody confusion before clouds of English arrows, shot by leather-jerkined fellows of no breeding at all, the armored knight became an anachronism. Gunpowder would soon have made him so, if the cloth-yard arrow had not.

Cavalry could never be overwhelming again, as important as it remained. It had to become again, as it had been before the age of knights in armor, flexible, swift, evasive, capable of outflanking an enemy instead of riding him down. And so speed, rather than weight-carrying ability, became the criterion of a war horse. It is as simple as that, if you compress a few centuries.

There were, of course, many light horses in England. But they were small (under 14 hands for the most part), and incapable of bearing up under the grueling use. What was needed was a type roughly as tall as the heavy breeds but considerably lighter, with good bone, strong back, powerful muscle—a horse which would combine speed with stamina. It is no wonder that England turned to the Arabian, the Turk, and the Barb, for since the first crusades the reputation of the "desert horse" for speed and endurance was well known. As early as the reign of Henry VIII there was a royal stud, and if it slipped

under Edward VI, it was revived under Elizabeth, and most of the subsequent monarchs continued to interest themselves in the breeding of horses. It is only one more link in the tradition that, in the year this pamphlet is published, horses from the stable of George VI have won four out of the five great English classics for 3-year-olds.

To put the matter very briefly, Eastern horses of all sorts—Arabs, Barbs, and Turks—were brought into England in increasing numbers. It was fashion and it was good sound sense. With increasing numbers of horses whose boast was speed, trials of this speed became more numerous and more interesting. There was racing at Chester in the sixteenth century under Henry VIII. There was a race track, definitely laid out, at Doncaster in 1595. Cromwell issued a proclamation in 1654 forbidding racing for six months, apparently fearing that the race courses might become Cavalier meeting places. By the time of Charles II, racing had gained sufficient bulk and prominence that it is sometimes said that "real racing" began in his reign. This is to ignore the fact that racing never began in recorded history; it has existed from the start. But if a semi-modern starting place is desired, the years of the Restoration (1660-1688) will do as well as any.

It should be understood that the racing of the seventeenth and eighteenth centuries was very far from racing as it exists today. Prize money in England, as late as 1725, did not amount to more than $35,000. The races were usually matches between two horses, and it was very seldom that more than three or four contested the same race. The contests were usually decided in heats of various lengths, two or more heats being necessary to determine the winner.

Early Conditions Weights were much higher than at present; in 1739, by royal proclamation, no races could be run at Newmarket with less than 12 stone, or 168 pounds. Horses were allowed to mature completely before they raced; it was considered that 4-year-olds were about the youngest that could be run, and most authorities favored waiting a year or so longer. There were no grandstands in the modern sense; except for a sprinkling of local country people, who might be on foot, it was watched from horseback or from carriages. Since there were no admissions, and no source of revenue for the tracks, the prizes were usually the result of private stakes, though to assist in improving the horses the government put up a series of "king's plates." There were no tracks in the modern sense; races were run over convenient fields or commons with stakes marking the courses. A rope from stake to stake was the ancestor of the rails which surround modern tracks.

But although racing went on in considerable volume, and although many horses were bred in

A study of the head of Silver Thrush, a high-class racer in India, but in appearance more typical of the Arab than the Thoroughbred. Distinguishing characteristics are the concave profile, short, close-set ears, large, round, intelligent eyes, firm nostrils, delicately modeled muzzle. It was from the Arab and similar breeds that the modern Thoroughbred descended, increasing in size, strength, and speed during the descent.

From a painting by Martin Stainforth.

England, neither racing nor breeding became a matter of public record until well into the eighteenth century. Many of the breed-

Beginning of Records

ers kept their own records—Cuthbert Routh's stud book from 1718 to 1752 is extant; so is that of the Duke of Ancaster at the same period. Prospero d'Osma made an inventory of the royal stud of Elizabeth, at the behest of the Earl of Leicester. The stud book of Lord Godolphin was apparently something of a model of its time, for when Reginald Heber published a suggestion for a stud book, in his racing calendar for 1756, it followed the Godolphin records closely.

All these records, however, were private. And though the results of many races are known, and the records of many individual horses have been preserved, there is no way of getting to all of English racing before 1727. In that year John Cheny began the publication, by subscription, of "An Historical List or Account of all the Horse-Matches run, and of all the Plates and Prizes run for in England (of the value of ten pounds or upwards) in 1727." This was taken up after Cheny's death by Reginald Heber, whose first volume came in 1751. For 1769 through 1772 the same work went on, under the title of the *Sporting Calendar*, published by William Tuting and Thomas Fawconer, and in 1773 it passed to James Weatherby and it remained in that family until 1902, when it was purchased by the Jockey Club,

for which it is still published by Weatherby and Sons. It is, of course, the official organ of the Jockey Club; unofficially it always had almost the same authority.

Heber had opposition from John Pond, who published a rival "Sporting Kalendar" from 1751 through 1757. There was a B. Walker who attempted to run against Tuting and Fawconer, but he gave up after two years. There was quite a battle in 1772, involving Tuting, Fawconer, and Weatherby; there is no use raising the merits of the controversy now. In summary, Tuting left Fawconer and went with Weatherby, and then Tuting died in 1773, leaving Weatherby in possession of the field. Fawconer continued to issue annual volumes until he died in 1777.

In the foreword to the volume of 1727, Cheny remarked that, though certain gentlemen had suggested the desirability of including pedigrees,

Pedigrees

he had been unable to do so, and hinted that he might include them in subsequent volumes. Actually it was not until 1743 that he did so. The first pedigree given, for reasons which will appear presently, is here transcribed entire, except that Cheny's somewhat original ideas of capitalization have not been followed.

Bucephalus was bred by Mr. Aislabie himself, and got by Robinson Crusoe, son of Jigg, son of the Byerly Turk.

His dam was got by Snake, his grandam by Hautboy.

Robinson Crusoe was bred by Mr. Robinson of Richmond. His dam was called Bastard, she was descended from a noted mare called Old Wilks, which was bred by the late Mr. Wilks, of Yorkshire, out of a Darcy or Sedbury mare and Old Hautboy.

The grandsire of Bucephalus, called Jigg, was bred by Sir. Roger Moystin of Wales; his dam was got by Spanker, son of the Darcy Yellow Turk.

I have been assured by a Person of Rank and great Honour that the horse called by sportsmen the Byerly Turk, which horse (as observed) was the great grandsire of Bucephalus, was in fact an Arabian.

He was Capt. Byerly's charging horse in Ireland in the time of King William's wars, and (as well known) proved afterward a very excellent stallion.

Snake (which got the dam of Bucephalus) never was a running horse; he was render'd incapable therof by a tumorous swelling that attended him in his youth, and from the supposition that the same was the effect of a sting or bite from some venemous reptile, he was called Snake.

He was bred by Mat. Lister, Esq., of Lincolnshire, out of a daughter of Hautboy and the Stradling or Lister Turk, brought into England by the Duke of Berwick from the siege of Buda, in the reign of King Charles the Second.

King Charles the Second sent abroad the Master of the Horse (which some say was a late Sir Christopher Wyvil; others the late Sir John Fenwick) in order to procure a number of foreign high-bred horses and mares for breeding, and the mares, thus produced by the said king's interest, and brought to England (as also many of their offspring) have for that reason, been called Royal Mares, one of which was the dam of Hautboy.

Spanker (as observ'd) was got by the Darcy Yellow Turk.

His dam was called the old Morocco Mare, because got by a Morocco Barb, which Barb was the property of the Lord General Fairfax.

Spanker's grandam was called Bald Peg, which was bred by the Lord Fairfax, out of a Barb mare and an Arabian.

Cheny goes on, for approximately two more pages, to list other horses got by the stallions named in this pedigree.

Several points in this pedigree are to be insisted upon.

First, line after line goes back to an Eastern horse, whether Arab, Barb, or Turk.

Second, very few of these are named. The designation of Spanker's dam as "the old Morocco mare" means nothing; all unnamed mares by the same stallion would be called the same thing. Much the same can be said of the "old Wilks mare," which got her name from that of her breeder. Only two of the 13 mares in the pedigree as given could be positively identified.

Third, there is no mention of racing performance anywhere in the pedigree, except that two stallions, Snake and Hautboy, are mentioned as never running. Probably, in many cases, such incompleteness was unavoidable, even in 1743.

Fourth, the story of Charles II and his royal mares is strictly fiction, as was demonstrated by the eminent English scholar C. M. Prior.

It is from Cheny that James Weatherby, Jr., drew chiefly when he published, in 1791, *An Introduction to a General Stud Book*, though he drew from private records as far as they were available, and of course from many minor sources. He drew also from Pick's *Histori-*

The First Stud Book

cal Account of Yorkshire Races, a reasonably complete history of racing in the shire of York from 1709 to 1785. This book, not published until 1786, also contained a collection of pedigrees. It had been felt for many years that a general stud book was desirable, to prevent falsification of pedigrees and to eliminate honest mistakes as well.

Weatherby's introductory volume could of course go no further back than his sources, and consequently it is only occasionally that he records foals of years earlier than 1750. A few appear, however, going back as early as 1711.

That this book was filled with mistakes was unavoidable. Weatherby himself was so sure of it that in addition to several pages of "Errata and Addenda," he printed several blank pages under the same head, in order that owners of the book might write in what additional errors were discovered. But it represented a start, and it adopted the form which the stud books of all countries have preserved, almost unchanged, to the present day. Volume I of the *General Stud Book* appeared two years later, in 1793. The introduction contained 207 pages; Volume I, in its final edition, has more than 400. It was revised in 1803, 1808, 1827, 1858, and finally on its one-hundredth anniversary, 1891. The book still remains the property of the Weatherby family, Volume 29, issued in 1941, being the latest.

And now we are prepared to answer, strictly from an English point of view, the first question, "What is a Thoroughbred?" It is a horse which traces back in all branches, without flaw, to animals registered in the *General Stud Book*.

It may have in its veins the blood of Arab, Barb, Turk, galloway, Scotch pony, cart horse, draft breed, Highland Dun, and heaven knows what else, though it will always be predominantly Arabian, Barb, or Turk. But it is descended from horses which, in the main, proved themselves on the race course, and whose descendants have proved themselves on the same testing ground, for approximately 250 years. Originally no more than the intention of being a race horse was needed to obtain entry, but the *General Stud Book* is now a closed circle; no blood not already in it can be admitted.

To put it another way, the Thoroughbred is a horse descended, in all lines, from ancestors which were bred and trained for racing for approximately 250 years, and which were selected as breeding stock primarily by their performance.

Perhaps a rather summary distinction among the three Eastern breeds which made up the great bulk of the ancestry of the Thoroughbred is in order. The Arab came from Arabia, of course,

Eastern Sources

from a breed which was cultivated by the Bedouins for centuries. A pleasant myth is that Mohammed shut all the horses he could get into an enclosure without water for a few days, then released them in sight of a stream. As the horses thundered away to water, he had a trumpeter blow a battle call. Most of the herd went sensibly on, a few turned obediently back, and from these few the great Arabian strains were bred. The story is valuable only to indicate how long the Arab has been bred and for how many centuries the necessities of war have shaped his destiny. Physically the Arabian horse, mostly bay, stood about 14½ hands high at the withers, weighed from 800 to 1,000 pounds, had hard, dense bone, and a short back, and the general ability to carry weight for long distances under adverse conditions.

The Barb got his name from Barbary (North

4

Bert Clark Thayer.

Leading money-winner of the world is Calumet Farm's WHIRLAWAY, foaled in 1938 and winner of $548,461 through November 11, 1942. His sire, *Blenheim II, won the English Derby in 1930. Whirlaway set a new time record when he won the Kentucky Derby of 1941, finishing with a smothering stretch rush as his sire had done in the Derby at Epsom Downs.

Africa), whence he was brought into Spain by the Moors. A bit coarser than the Arab, he was of about the same size, and was also known for his speed and endurance. The Turk, a mixture of Arab, Persian, and other Asiatic breeds, was somewhat larger, standing from 15 to 16 hands high, and was more like the modern Thoroughbred in size and general appearance than the others. He came from Turkey, of course. Fundamentally, of course, these were all variations of light horses, springing from common ancestors.

But not all of the early importations came with their proper credentials. The Lister or Stradling Turk, which was brought to England in the time of James I, was a part of the spoils of Buda. The Belgrade Turk was taken when Prince Eugene beat the Turks at Belgrade under the reign of Queen Anne. A good many others were the prizes of war, and they got their designation from the country whence they came. That is, a horse bought in Constantinople, or taken from the Turks, was pretty sure to be called a Turk, regardless of his actual ancestry, and an Arab brought from Spain or Barbary was likely to be considered a Barb. The difference among the three breeds, though they held in general, were not always enough to identify individuals beyond question.

Of the many Eastern stallions introduced into England it is necessary to notice only a few, though it should be remembered that the others, too, had their part in making up the breed. However, only three have male lines extant today. The earliest of these is the Byerly Turk, mentioned by Cheny as "Capt. Byerly's charging horse" in the Irish wars. There is a story that he also was captured from the Turks,

Foundation Sires

but little else is known of him. He seems to have been foaled about 1679, and to have been in the stud as late as 1698.

The Godolphin Arabian was foaled about 1724. He stood about 15 hands high, or an inch less, and several stories are told of him. According to one he was a present to Louis XIV of France by the Emperor of Morocco. Another is that he was stolen and taken to Paris. He got to England, at all events, and eventually came to the stud of the Earl of Godolphin. There is some argument that he was a Barb and not an Arabian, but since this is chiefly based on surviving paintings, it seems idle.

The Darley Arabian has a slightly more certain origin. He was bought in Aleppo by Thomas Darley and sent to his father in England, arriving in 1704, at the age of four. He stood about 15 hands high. There are records in the stud book which show him to have had foals as late as 1735, but these are probably in error.

One other might be mentioned. At about the time of Queen Anne, a grey stallion called Alcock's Arabian was brought to England, and he seems to be responsible for the color of virtually all of the grey Thoroughbreds now living. It should be familiar to the student that a grey horse must have at least one grey parent, and if the greys are followed through a pedigree, they will, with the scantiest of exceptions, go to the Alcock Arabian, though some of them will also trace, also in an unbroken sequence of greys, to the Brownlow Turk.

The other three left more sizeable legacies to the Turf. Every Thoroughbred in the world today traces in male line to the Darley Arabian, the Godolphin Arabian, or the Byerly Turk.

(Male line: son to sire to grandsire, etc.) In modern pedigrees, however, male lines are traced only to three descendants of these horses. The Darley Arabian is the great-great-grandsire of Eclipse (1764); the Byerly Turk is the great-great-grandsire of Herod (1758); and the Godolphin Arabian is the grandsire of Matchem (1748). No other branches of the original male lines exist, and modern horsemen trace pedigrees only to Herod, Matchem, or Eclipse, in male line.

Male Lines

As the sires of the Thoroughbred race were few, so were their dams. Bruce Lowe, who probably did more work on female lines than anyone else, and to less purpose, estimated that there were fewer than 100 original mares in the stud book. Of these, only about 40 of the tap-root mares have persisted in tail-female line. There are other foundation mares in America, Australia, and elsewhere, which may descend from these but whose pedigrees cannot be traced exactly, but this aspect of the subject will be discussed elsewhere.

Female Families

Most of the tap-root mares are unnamed, and are designated by the name of the sire or their owner, as Burton's Barb mare, Bustler mare, A Royal Mare, Mare by T. Gascoigne's Foreign Horse, Sister to Old Merlin, etc., in the original records. Prior has pointed out that only three, Queen Anne's Moonah Barb mare (imported *in utero*), the dam of Dodsworth, and a mare owned by Lord Arlington, have provable Eastern origins. It should be mentioned that the "Layton Barb mare" does not indicate the mare was a Barb, but that she was sired by a Barb.

The foundation of the Thoroughbred, in the main, consisted in breeding imported stallions to native mares, and in breeding the daughters of such matings either to other imported stallions, or to such sons and male-line descendants of imported stallions as had shown conspicuous merit, with the result that in the course of a few generations the native blood had been obscured by the imported. The rage for imported stallions died out about a century after it began, probably because the horses which were being bred in England, particularly for racing and on a basis of performance, became more successful than miscellaneous and unraced stock which was brought in. From about 1750 forward, not a great deal of Arabian or other Eastern blood was imported, and the progress of English breeding consisted in mating the most successful mares to the most successful sires. That is, inferior stock was discarded, the best retained.

In the subsequent 200 years, the race horse has grown a good deal physically, and the descendants of the original Arabs and Barbs are now considerably taller than their ancestors; taking the average of the breed, the Thoroughbred's height is probably almost 16 hands, or five feet, four inches, measured at the withers. In 1873 Admiral Rous declared: "The stature of Thoroughbred stock has increased since the year 1700 an inch every 25 years, and whereas the average size of horses then was 13 hands 3 inches, the average is now 15 hands 2 inches, and they can carry twice as much weight as 100 years ago." (These figures are probably not strictly accurate.) The modern Thoroughbred has grown in speed also, and can run away and hide from the modern Arabian. Within the last year the bar has been raised against Arabian horses, and these can no longer be admitted to the *American Stud Book*. In a few brief words, the modern Thoroughbred

Physical Progress

is the result of selective breeding, over two centuries, for speed and stamina, as these are tested on the race course, and he has improved materially over the stock upon which his race was built.

The history of the American Thoroughbred parallels that of the English rather exactly except for dates. It must be remembered that the settlers in Virginia, Maryland, and the Carolinas, where racing appeared first, were Englishmen, and were acquainted with English horses and racing practices. Since early newspapers are almost the only source of the records, it is not known exactly when races were first run. In New York, where horses were brought as early as 1625, but apparently with no respect to bloodlines (they were probably from Flanders), there was racing on Long Island at least as far back as 1665. Early records show races in the Carolinas in 1734, in Virginia in 1739, in Maryland in 1745. Presumably these were very informal affairs.

American Beginnings

But Governor Ogle introduced racing, "between pedigreed horses, in the English style," at Annapolis in 1745, and this date may be said to mark, approximately, the beginning of Thoroughbred breeding and racing in North America. By tradition, the first Thoroughbred importation was the stallion *Bully Rock, or *Bulle Rock, in 1730, but as he was 21 years old when he arrived and as there were of course few opportunities for him to be mated with mares of racing heritage, his connection with later pedigrees is almost nil. The records show a few other importations before 1745, and in 1747 Governor Ogle brought over *Spark and the celebrated mare *Queen Mab at the same time. *Traveller (Morton's) arrived in 1748, established an enduring reputation. In 1750 Col. Benjamin Tasker imported the famous mare *Selima, which proved herself an outstanding racer, one of the most distinguished and lasting sources of excellence in American pedigrees, and the basis of innumerable arguments as to her ancestry (arguments now settled at last, but not in keeping with the *American Stud Book*). Governor Sharpe, also of Maryland, brought over *Othello in 1755, and *Janus and *Fearnought came a few years later. The foundations of the American Thoroughbred were now laid.

The Revolution interrupted the growth of Thoroughbred breeding, but as soon as it was over the stream of importations was reestablished, and by this time the stallions and mares being brought from England found many American-bred mates which had been tested on the race courses. Racing and the Thoroughbred gained rapidly in the postwar years, and there were many famous horses in the years from 1790 forward. As civilization moved westward across the Appalachians the Thoroughbred went with it, and it was not many years before Tennessee and Kentucky were breeding horses worthy of competition with the best along the Atlantic side of the mountains.

The record of this growth is much too long to attempt even the briefest summary here, and its detail is not collected anywhere. We know a great deal of the names, pedigrees, and exploits of the best horses of these early years, but such information has been pieced together from many sources and is nowhere found in a comprehensive reference series. The first continuous recording of American racing begins with the *American Turf Register and Sporting Magazine*, the first issue of which was published in

Printed Records

Baltimore in September, 1829, by John Stuart Skinner, good friend of Francis Scott Key, author of the *Star Spangled Banner.* The recorded racing results of subsequent years are available in printed form, though the volumes covering the years before 1875 are rare, and in some cases all but unobtainable.

The *American Stud Book* began with the publication of Volumes 1 and 2 by Sanders D. Bruce in 1873 (after the abortive publication of Volume 1 in 1868), though several other attempts at a stud book had been made. These volumes were revised in 1884, but they still contain innumerable errors revealed by later research. The *American Stud Book* was purchased in 1896 by The Jockey Club, and all American registrations are now conducted through that organization. The latest volume is number 17. In method of organization this series, like the stud books of all countries, follows Weatherby's original *Introduction,* in which foals were arranged chronologically under the names of their dams.

In America, as elsewhere, all male lines go back to Herod, Matchem, and Eclipse. But there are many female families not recognized by the *General Stud Book,* though they were recognized until 1913, when the distinction was hit upon as a means of removing American horses from competition in world markets. As a result, many lines which got into the *General Stud Book* before the bars were put up continue in English pedigrees, and have to be explained away, now and then. To put the matter unkindly, the *General Stud Book* gets along nicely with the "impurities" introduced before 1913, but will not accept the same lines now, though they have been improved by two or three more generations of selective breeding.

Non-English "Impurities"

In point of fact, the American tap-roots that have persisted probably have a better case than the English tap-roots. By 1750 the Thoroughbred was a fairly well defined breed. The sires of the American mares, in most instances, were imported stallions of known ancestry and merit, rather than unidentified Arabs and Barbs whose racing class was and remained untested. The men who bred them were trying to get race horses, and would hardly have set about this with mares from slower or heavier breeds. Better mares were available for purchase in 1750 than in England a century earlier, for purchase of Eastern mares was a near-impossibility in the early days of the Thoroughbred.

It will be remembered that at the time the earliest American tap-root mares were foaled, there was as yet no stud book in England or elsewhere. Considering how many records of English horses of the same period are not available (many of the horses in Cheny's volumes cannot be traced), it is not surprising that unnamed mares, which either did not race, or of whose racing there is no record, failed to get across the Atlantic with their pedigrees. This is not to insist that all American tap-roots spring from imported racing stock. Presumably most of them did, and possibly some came from lower sources, as did the earliest English mares.

However, the logic of the owners of the *General Stud Book* is not particularly important. The history of breeding in the United States and the history of breeding in England is much the same, a century apart: imported stallions were bred to what mares were available, the daughters of these were bred to the best stallions that could be had, and the breed moved on, with the race course as the testing ground for breeding probabilities. Any "cold" blood in either country is now so far back in pedigrees that it may be considered negligible.

FRIAR ROCK was a power in the August Belmont stable in 1916, being the leading 3-year-old of that year. Especially to be noted are his short cannons, straight hind leg, powerful muscular organization, and commanding carriage. He was one of the finest stayers of his day; in his last race he beat Roamer and The Finn in the 1¾-mile Saratoga Cup.

R. L. McClure.

DISTRIBUTION: The Progress of the Thoroughbred and Organized Racing from England to the Rest of the World.

FROM England the Thoroughbred and the racing which goes with him have spread to virtually all the great centers of population, and many of the small ones, in the more civilized sections of the world, the principal exceptions being accounted for mostly by physical obstacles or economic insufficiency. Not only the English blood, but the English pattern of racing has spread everywhere, and virtually every great racing country has its routine modeled after that of England to as great an extent as local conditions allow. Virtually every country in continental Europe, for instance, has (or had, before the war) its approximations of the five English classics for 3-year-olds, the Two Thousand Guineas and One Thousand Guineas (for fillies) at a mile, the Derby and Oaks (for fillies) at a mile and a half, and the St. Leger, at a mile and three-quarters.

British Pattern

Next to the racing in the British Isles, that in France occupies the most important position in Europe, as seen from a world point of view. Germany and Italy likewise have a long tradition of racing and breeding, and so had Austria and Russia. As a matter of fact, if we except The Hague, there is hardly a capital city in Europe which was a stranger to racing before the beginning of the current world war, and even in the midst of the most destructive war in history the sport goes on in England, France, Germany, Italy, and possibly in other countries.

Europe

India, Burma, Ceylon, the Federated Malay States had well organized racing, and China had much of the sport, though it was largely without benefit of Thoroughbred blood. Before the war (possibly now) racing was a very popular sport in Japan, and the government there had taken a leading part in popularizing it, since Japan, being more militaristic, was even more acutely aware than other countries of the Thoroughbred's role in effecting the improvement of horses for military purposes. South Africa has numerous race courses and a well developed breeding industry.

Asia, Africa

South America is almost as completely devoted to the Thoroughbred as Europe, and some of the most beautiful race courses in the world are found there. Argentina, Uruguay, Chile, and Brazil have much racing which compares favorably with the best in the United States. During the last few years some of the best horses racing in North America have been importations from south of the equator, and this has been one of the many factors which have served to bring the two continents of the western hemisphere into closer contact with one another. Only recently the stud book authorities of the principal South American nations have declared their intention to accept the *American Stud Book* and to overthrow their former strict adherence to the *General Stud Book* of England.

South America

If we move across the southern Pacific to Australia and New Zealand we find some of the most enthusiastic racing audiences in the entire world, and some of the largest Thoroughbred breeding operations. Australia's greatest race, the Melbourne Cup, a two-mile handicap in which the weights allotted to outstanding horses frequently range up to 140 pounds, is one of the most famous contests among horses in the world. The British enthusiasm for the ancient sport is no less apparent in the Dominion of Canada, where a comparatively light population finds half a dozen very active centers of racing activity.

Down Under and Over

Racing in Mexico for many years has been largely an appendage of racing in the United States, with the scene of actual operations moved across the border merely for the sake of privileges which would not be allowed in the States. But a magnificent new racing plant is now being constructed at Mexico City with the hope of establishing the sport there on as sound a basis and with as high traditions as elsewhere.

Nor is this the whole picture of the extent of Thoroughbred racing. It flourishes in many islands, in countries difficult to reach, and in one form or another, under almost any conditions which it can tolerate. Racing in Cuba has long been regarded as being of a piece with that in the United States, but there is racing also in Puerto Rico, the Virgin Islands, Jamaica, Madagascar, and even in Mauritius, a tiny island in the Indian Ocean five hundred miles east of Madagascar. The Isthmus of Panama has one of the most active race courses in the western hemisphere.

It hardly seems feasible to attempt a comparison of racing in different countries, except to say that the sport in the United States dwarfs that of other countries in the matter of number of racing days, number of races, and money. In the United States approximately 13,500 races were being run each year before the war began, including about two hundred steeplechase events. No other country has half as many races a year.

Quantity, Quality

But numbers, used in such a comparison, could be deceiving, for it is not the number of races for cheap horses that determines the value of the Turf in the improvement of the breed of horses, but rather the class and proportion of the best races, and the extent to which the unworthy are discarded from the breed. In actual practice there is something of a disadvantage, as far as the improvement of horses is concerned, in the extent of American racing, which is so vast that it maintains thousands of horses which in any other major country would be in greater peril of being discarded entirely from the ranks of registered Thoroughbreds.

In the United States racing is widely scattered geographically, though the greatest concentration is along the Atlantic seaboard. In 1941, for example, within the borders of the United States there were 13,916 races, with purses of $16,380,080. New York, Maryland, Florida, Rhode Island, Delaware, and Massachusetts accounted for 5,181 of the races and $7,857,807 of the money. Since this represents 37 per cent of the racing and 48 per cent of the money, it is obvious that this is also the richest racing.

Among the States

There is a full season of racing in Illinois, that State ranking third in the nation in number of races and amount of purses. California, before the war stopped racing there abruptly, had a year-round circuit, ranking first in number of races, second in money distributed in purses. These figures are for 1941; California was first in 1938 and 1939, but lost her ascendancy to New York, in which there is no minor racing at all.

The five New York tracks, together with Santa Anita and Hollywood Parks in California, Pimlico in Maryland, Arlington and Washington Parks in Illinois, made up the 10 leading American race tracks ranked by the average amount of money given daily in purses in 1941. Of these, Belmont Park is the highest.

It may seem odd to a newcomer that Kentucky, usually thought of first in connection with race horses, appears in none of these rankings. The fact is that Kentucky, preeminent in breeding Thoroughbreds, has no great amount of racing within her own borders. In 1941 there were 21 days of racing at Keeneland, 32 at Churchill Downs, including only 402 races, and this was all the racing in the State, except for the cheaper sport at Dade Park, toward the western end of the State.

In 1941 there was legalized and recognized racing in the following 19 states, which are given in the order of their total purse distribution, as listed in the *American Racing Manual:* New York, California, Illinois, Maryland, Florida, Rhode Island, Massachusetts, Kentucky, Ohio, Michigan, New Hampshire, West Virginia, Delaware, Washington, Arkansas, Nebraska, Arizona, Louisiana, and Nevada. New Mexico also had racing on a modest scale, not accounted for in the *Manual.* The latest comer of these is Delaware, which began racing in 1937. Racing has been legal for several years in New Jersey, but there had been no recent racing there until 1942.

In Texas racing laws were repealed in 1937, and Missouri, which had extra-legal racing, gave it up in the same year. Hunt racing, which has many enthusiastic devotees, flourishes in several states, notably Virginia, Maryland, Pennsylvania, New Jersey, New York, and the Carolinas.

In the breeding of Thoroughbreds, Kentucky is well at the top, producing more high-class horses (but not more horses) than the other 47 states together. Breeding is carried on with considerable volume and success also in Maryland, Virginia, New Jersey, California, and Texas, and horses are also bred in some numbers in Ohio, Illinois, Washington, and Tennessee. Elsewhere Thoroughbred nurseries are only occasional, though there is probably not a state in which some Thoroughbreds are not foaled.

Breeding in U. S. A.

In production of high-class horses Virginia, which cradled the American Thoroughbred, ranks second to Kentucky. But recent years have seen such an expansion of breeding that top horses are beginning to appear from sections which formerly were scarcely thought of in connection with the Thoroughbred—horses, for example, such as Mioland from Oregon, the champion sprinter Doublrab, which was foaled nearly as far north in Illinois as Mioland was in Oregon, and the excellent colt Valdina Orphan, foaled on the vast Valdina Farms not far from San Antonio, Texas. Traditionally it has long been accepted that the limestone soils and temperate, changeable climates of Kentucky and Virginia gave these States and a few others a considerable advantage in the production of race horses, but the spread of breeding operations is demonstrating that good horses may be bred in many other sections, provided those sections have good breeding stock.

An ideal hunter and show horse type, showing extraordinary quality. The head of Iron Master, famous as a hunter and show jumper, as modeled in bronze by the noted sculptor Herbert Haseltine.

Peter A. Juley and Son.

PEDIGREE: The Form and Language of Representing Thoroughbred Ancestry; Outmoded Theories; the Search for Correlations.

BY pedigree we mean simply ancestry, or the record thereof. It may consist merely of the names of the sire and dam of a horse. Frequently it is written in the following form:

Alsab, b. c., 1939 [bay colt, foaled in 1939], by Good Goods out of Winds Chant, by Wildair out of Eulogy, by Fair Play out of *St. Eudora, by St. Simon. . . .

The asterisk (*) is used in many American publications, including the *American Stud Book,* to indicate a horse foaled abroad and imported to North America.

A familiar form of showing the ancestry of race horses is the tabulated pedigree, like that of Whirlaway shown below. The sire of Whirlaway is *Blenheim II. (When he won the Derby in England in 1930, he was plain Blenheim; the asterisk and numeral were added when he came to America, the asterisk to denote the fact that he was imported, the numeral to distinguish him from another horse named Blenheim.) The dam of Whirlaway is Dustwhirl. *Blenheim II is by Blandford out of Malva; Dustwhirl by Sweep out of Ormonda. And so on, until all the ancestors of Whirlaway through five generations are shown. This form can be used for any required number of generations of ancestors.

The form in which the tabulated pedigree fans out suggests the origin of the word, which comes through Middle English from the Old French *pie de crue,* which in turn derived from the Latin *pes* (foot) and *grus* (crane). *Pie de crue,* or

pied de crue, as modern French has it, was an expression to describe a three-line symbol indicating descent in old genealogical records.

It would perhaps be well to explain a few of the terms which have come to have specialized meanings in this connection. The sire is, of course, the male parent; the grandsire, unless otherwise specified or suggested, is the sire's sire; the great-grandsire is the grandsire's sire, etc. The dam is the female parent. Her dam is called the grandam or second dam, whose mother is referred to as the third dam; and so on back. The dam's sire is usually referred to as the maternal grandsire, and in the use of the unqualified term grandsire it is usually the paternal grandsire which is meant.

Terms and Special Usage

The sire, grandsire, great-grandsire, and so on constitute the horse's *male line.* In the case of Whirlaway the male line (sometimes called tail-male line) goes through *Blenheim II, Blandford, Swynford, John o' Gaunt, etc., and can be extended back 14 generations (if we begin the count with *Blenheim II) to Eclipse, one of the three patriarchs to which the male lines of all Thoroughbreds now living can be traced. Ordinarily, if the extension of the pedigree is made along the lower edge of the pedigree, through dam, second dam, third dam, etc., we call it a *family* rather than a line. (This isn't the only thing in Thoroughbred breeding for which no very good reason can be assigned.) Such an extension, however, is occasionally called a tail-female line.

Older pedigree forms frequently stated that a horse was *got* by such and such a stallion out of such and such a mare. From this comes the still common practice of calling the sons and daughters of a stallion his *get*—not his gets, as an occasional commentator misapprehends the word. The progeny of a mare are usually called her

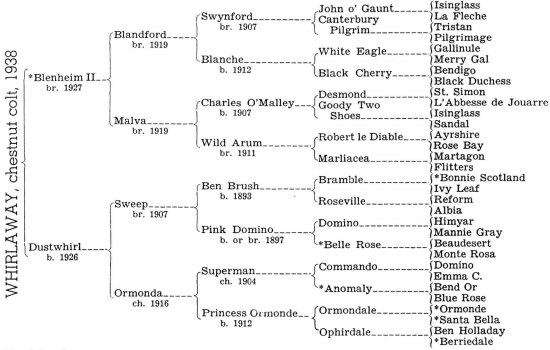

WHIRLAWAY, chestnut colt, 1938

*Blenheim II, br. 1927
  Blandford, br. 1919
    Swynford, br. 1907
      John o' Gaunt — Isinglass / La Fleche
      Canterbury Pilgrim — Tristan / Pilgrimage
    Blanche, b. 1912
      White Eagle — Gallinule / Merry Gal
      Black Cherry — Bendigo / Black Duchess
  Malva, br. 1919
    Charles O'Malley, b. 1907
      Desmond — St. Simon / L'Abbesse de Jouarre
      Goody Two Shoes — Isinglass / Sandal
    Wild Arum, br. 1911
      Robert le Diable — Ayrshire / Rose Bay
      Marliacea — Martagon / Flitters
Dustwhirl, b. 1926
  Sweep, br. 1907
    Ben Brush, b. 1893
      Bramble — *Bonnie Scotland / Ivy Leaf
      Roseville — Reform / Albia
    Pink Domino, b. or br. 1897
      Domino — Himyar / Mannie Gray
      *Belle Rose — Beaudesert / Monte Rosa
  Ormonda, ch. 1916
    Superman, ch. 1904
      Commando — Domino / Emma C.
      *Anomaly — Bend Or / Blue Rose
    Princess Ormonde, b. 1912
      Ormondale — *Ormonde / *Santa Bella
      Ophirdale — Ben Holladay / *Berriedale

No. 8 family.
* Imported.

10

produce; and if, in a sale catalogue, a mare is referred to as a producer, it means that at least one of her produce is a winner on a recognized track. By the same token, it is common practice, in compiling pedigrees and sale catalogues, to refer to a stallion as a sire only after at least one of his get has become a winner.

If a mare has two colts by the same sire they are, of course, brothers. If she has two colts by different sires, they are half-brothers. But two colts by the same sire out of different mares are not called half-brothers; they are, of course, just as much half-brothers as two sons of the same mare, but with horse breeders the term is limited arbitrarily to indicate the relationship on the dam's side. Sometimes horses with the same grandparents, but not with the same parents, are referred to as brothers in blood. Sometimes such expressions as three-quarter-brothers, or seven-eighths-brothers are heard, but the use of these terms is not recommended, as their meanings may be obscure.

In Thoroughbred practice, a *colt* is an entire (that is, not castrated) male less than five years old; when he reaches the age of five, he is called a *horse.* Similarly, fillies are called *mares* when they reach the age of five (or earlier, if bred to a stallion). The word *horse* is also used in its broader application to include mares and geldings (castrated males), but the word *colt* is not used when a young female is meant.

For all its excellent arrangement and the ease with which it can be read, the usual tabulated pedigree of a Thoroughbred horse is singularly bare of important information. Sometimes the colors and foaling dates of the near generations of ancestors are given, but these items can scarcely be said to be of importance to the breeder or the student, unless, indeed, he happens to be concerned with the inheritance of coat color as an exercise in genetics. Boiled down to its essence, the tabulated pedigree consists of names of ancestors. Through long acquaintance with these names the breeder learns to set values upon them and, sometimes, to associate fairly definite qualities with them, and hence arrives at a nebulous appraisal of the pedigree. Pedigrees of Standardbred (trotting and pacing) horses are never tabulated without a "record" appended to each name, indicating the horse's speed at the standard mile distance, wherever such records are available. Unfortunately there is no system of symbols yet devised by which the class of a Thoroughbred is indicated in his pedigree.

Contents of Pedigrees

The study, then, of Thoroughbred pedigrees has been based largely upon such generalizations or impressions as could be drawn from these names —their frequency, positions, or combinations in pedigrees of good horses. Since it has never been demonstrated that a breeder can increase appreciably his chances of turning out a high-class horse by following any of the "systems" derived from such studies, it is not necessary in this abbreviated summary to discuss any of them in detail. It is in order, however, to append a

One of the most brilliant fillies of the century was TOP FLIGHT, unbeaten as a 2-year-old, and now in the stud of her owner, C. V. Whitney.

One of the most uniformly successful stallions of recent years is *SIR GALLAHAD III, bred in France and imported to the United States. He has led the American sire list in four years, and has sired able stayers, brilliant sprinters.

few notes in order to familiarize the reader with some of the discussions occasionally encountered in the conversation and literature of Thoroughbred breeding.

A more or less generally accepted principle among breeders is that of nicks, or fortunate combinations of bloodlines. The supposition is made that a combination which has produced one or more good horses is more likely to produce other good horses than other combinations which have not turned out so fortunately. A successful combination is called a nick.

Nicks Thus Fair Play, which stood at the famous Nursery Stud of the late Major August Belmont until the Belmont estate horses were dispersed in 1925, got nearly all of his best offspring from mares which were daughters or granddaughters of *Rock Sand, which had preceded him as the premier sire at the Nursery Stud. After the Civil War the great nick was Lexington on mares by *Glencoe. Another famous nick, developed early in the present century, was the combination of Domino and Ben Brush blood. A combination which had outstanding success in England was that of Bend Or with mares by Macaroni.

So-called nicks are generally the result of propinquity or else they are sheer illusions, as in the case of Lexington and *Glencoe. A great many breeders, however, make it a practice to arrange matings so as to copy as nearly as possible the pattern of bloodlines in the pedigrees of good horses. No perceptible advantage is gained by this method.

An extension of the theory of nicks is the "dosage system" worked out in great detail by a French student of breeding, Lt. Col. J. Vuillier, who based his theory upon the greatly extended pedigrees of the great winners of the English Turf.

Dosage He noted that certain ancestors, through mild inbreeding, came to constitute a fairly stable percentage of the pedigrees of later generations. He computed the average proportion by which these ancestors contributed to the pedigrees of good horses, then advanced the doctrine that, in making matings, the breeder should attempt to approximate this average as closely as possible.

In recent years a considerable effort has been made to popularize this technique (such popularity, if achieved, would conceivably make it easier to sell English horses to the remainder of the world), but it is, fortunately, too complicated for the average breeder of Thoroughbreds to trouble himself with. The Aga Khan, one of Europe's most successful breeders, has largely followed the dosage system in making matings.

By considering the positions of names in pedigrees, breeders have also crystallized a few ideas of no special value. There is a very definite tendency, for instance, to seek out stallions which represent a "successful male line,"

Male Lines as a son, grandson, or great-grandson of *Teddy, Fair Play, or Broomstick, or even a descendant of a stallion foaled as long ago as Domino (1891) or Bend Or (1878). A similar tendency is seen in the preference of breeders for the daughters or granddaughters of some noted stallion because he had a reputation as a "great broodmare sire." Among horses thus classified in modern times *Star Shoot, Broomstick, Fair Play, Sweep are some notable examples. There is a disposition in some quarters to assume that a stallion, though he has failed as a sire, may be a "great broodmare sire" because he has good bloodlines. But, with exceptions too few to bother about, the best sires of runners are also the best sires of broodmares.

As a further involvement of the study of position, there are many breeders who believe that certain bloodlines, while they may give rise to good runners, are a disadvantage in the pedigree of a prospective sire. Of some sires it is occasionally declared that, while their daughters were good producers, their sons were failures at the stud. The prime "example" here is *Star Shoot.

The most complete system based upon the study of the position of names in pedigrees was that of Bruce Lowe, an Australian who was responsible for the "Figure Guide," the so-called **Bruce Lowe** Bruce Lowe system. This system, though it was based upon obviously specious reasoning, exerted much influence upon bloodstock breeding the world over, and though it has been thoroughly discredited it has left a few remnants of its basic ideas in the minds of breeders.

Mr. Lowe was principally concerned with female ancestors. All the classic winners of England were descended in tail-female from about 40 "original" mares. These "original" mares, or tap-roots, as they are frequently called, were assigned numbers according to the number of classic winners descended from them in tail-female, and all the tail-female descendants of each tap-root mare bore her family number, regardless of family numbers of the sires concerned. Thus the No. 1 family was the one which had the largest number of classic winners to its credit, No. 2 had the second largest number, etc. By this system of assigning numbers, it should be remembered that every foal takes the same family number as its dam.

By an ingenious elaboration of this material and a careful disregard of other material, Mr. Lowe promulgated the theory that each family was endowed with certain characteristics which were continued from generation to generation regardless of the male elements concerned in each

cross. The crowning creation of this collection of doctrines was the assumption that families No. 1, 2, 3, 4, and 5 were *running families*, and that No. 3, 8, 11, 12, and 14 were *sire families*. That is, according to Mr. Lowe and his followers, if one sought a good runner he needed only to emphasize the running families in making up pedigrees for prospective matings. But if he expected to breed a good sire, the prospective colt must either belong to a sire family or must be "inbred" to a sire family.

This latter doctrine has persisted in the minds of many breeders, who still insist that a sire will be a failure unless he comes of a sire family. In the main, however, they have modified their requirements and now look only for a good sire among the produce of the mares in the near background of the tail-female line.

On the matter of inbreeding there has been a great deal of study, but to no good end. The debate here has never settled to an issue. Suffice it to say that inbreeding among Thoroughbred horses is rarely practiced except in very mild degree, and that it provides no ascertainable advantage or disadvantage.

The various theories here briefly sketched have been mentioned only to dismiss them. They are a part of the background of Thoroughbred breeding, but nothing in any of **Futility of Systems** them has any practical value, except from the point of view of the salesman, who necessarily seeks to furnish his customers with whatever they want. Most of them so obviously ignore the principles made clear by modern genetics that it is no longer in order to investigate their dependability. But their dependability *has been* investigated on numerous occasions and found altogether wanting.

Ordinarily it would be considered unforgivably high-handed to make such a summary dismissal of issues which are still considered debatable in many quarters. We accept the responsibility of declaring the issues no longer debatable. In the office of the *Blood-Horse* there has been a long-term, sustained study of these questions, and to a lesser extent investigations have been carried on elsewhere. No evidence has been uncovered which

*A high-class broodmare was ROSE LEAVES, by Ballot, from whose 10 foals came six stakes winners, the last of which, DOGPATCH, is shown beside her as a four-day-old foal. Like two of her other stakes winners, he is by *Bull Dog.*

Joe H. Palmer.

would suggest that the breeder of race horses could gain an advantage through the application of any or all the theories mentioned.

Breeders talk of such things as nicks, male lines, families, etc., but in actual practice they tend to depend chiefly upon pedigrees and racing class to make their appraisals of stallions and broodmares. For making their matings, they depend largely upon convenience and conformation (in order to avoid obvious repetition of the same faults in sire and dam). Nicks of bloodlines are probably next in importance, in the mind of the average breeder.

Appraisal of Pedigrees

In appraising breeding stock—stallions and mares—it may be assumed that the importance which the breeder places upon the pedigree of a horse is in inverse proportion to the horse's racing class. That is, if the horse was definitely a high-class performer, his pedigree is more or less automatically considered to be good; but if the racing class was doubtful, or definitely low, the pedigree becomes, in proportion, more important in providing the horse with favorable credentials. Thus many of the stallions and most of the broodmares which are given opportunities in the stud are accorded their opportunities chiefly on the ground that their owners considered them to be well bred.

When we come to the technique of appraising pedigrees we have reached the most difficult, most debatable, most confused phase of Thoroughbred breeding. The standards of judgment vary so greatly from one individual breeder to another that few generalizations are possible. We may suppose that a good pedigree, in the mind of the average breeder, is one which shows relationship to good horses, and that the pedigree is "good" in proportion to the class of the relatives, the numbers of high-class relatives, and the nearness of the relationship. Thus a son of Man o' War or *Sir Gallahad III would be considered better bred on the sire's side than the son of an obscure sire, because Man o' War

Good and Bad

and *Sir Gallahad III, good performers themselves, are the sires of numerous high-class progeny and are themselves closely related to numerous high-class performers. On the "distaff side" of the pedigree the standards of judgment are, of course, the same, except that extra emphasis is usually placed upon two considerations, (1) whether the mare is by a "good broodmare sire," and (2) whether she "comes from a good producing family."

The tail-female descendants of *Filante, a mare imported as a yearling in 1917, offer an example of what the horseman means by a good family. In the following tabulation of *Filante's family, S indicates stakes winner, W winner. Only the more important horses in the family are accounted for.

*FILANTE, 1916, by Sardanapale
GAFFSMAN, 1923, by Jim Gaffney (S)
FILEMAKER, 1924, by *Ambassador IV (S)
FRISIUS, 1926, by *Star Hawk (S)
FLYING SPEAR, 1930, by *Sir Gallahad III (S)
FRESH FOX, 1932, by Gallant Fox (S)
FENELON, 1937, by *Sir Gallahad III (S)
FILOMAR, 1921, by *Omar Khayyam
  GAY O'MAR, 1927, by *Gay Ronald
    MYTHICAL KING, 1935, by *Pharamond II (S)
    JACOMAR, 1937, by Jack High (S)
FLIVVER, 1922, by Jim Gaffney
  CANFLI, 1928, by Campfire (S)
    HEELFLY, 1934, by Royal Ford (S)
  HIGH FLIGHT, 1929, by High Time
    LIBERTY FLIGHT, 1935, by Liberty Limited (S)
FLYING GAL, 1927, by *Sir Gallahad III (S)
  *BOSWELL, 1933, by Bosworth (S)
  GAINLY, 1935, by Gainsborough (S)
  *HYPNOTIST II, by Hyperion (S)
    PRECIPITOUS, 1939, by Precipitation (S)
FLYING SONG, 1931, by *Sir Gallahad III (W)
  APACHE, 1939, by *Alcazar (S)

Note: Descent is indicated by steps to the right. For instance, Filomar (like the others flush against the vertical line) is out of *Filante, Gay O'Mar is out of Filomar, and Mythical King and Jacomar are out of Gay O'Mar. Canfli and High Flight are out of Flivver.

The judgment of pedigree, however, frequently slips to the level of a rather slipshod appraisal of the mere names, without adequate checking to determine whether the connecting links between

ARIEL supplies an interesting contrast with the photograph on the preceding page. He is lengthy, extremely muscular, the muscle being rounded and thick rather than flat and long, and the development of his hindquarters is tremendous. A sprinter himself, his get are extremely fast within a limited distance.

Brownie Leach

the horse in question and the great names in the background were themselves possessed of distinction. Thus an occasional horse will be praised on the ground that he has "four crosses of Bend Or," or "five crosses of Galopin," or because he has some favorite combination of bloodlines, as Ben Brush and Domino.

The Big Names

If the first and second generation of ancestors (parents and grandparents) are skipped over lightly, the great majority of Thoroughbreds in America can be made out, in one way or another, to have very good pedigrees. The more remote crosses of any pedigree are very likely to be well stocked with some of the great names of the past, as Galopin, St. Simon, Isonomy, Hermit, Bend Or, Hampton, Stockwell, Newminster, etc., among English stallions, and Fair Play, Ben Brush, Domino, Hanover, and Lexington in America. These great names, while still looked upon as marks of distinction in a pedigree, have long since ceased to distinguish the very good from the no-good.

The principal reason for avoiding the judgment of race horses according to the remoter reaches of their pedigrees is the fact that such judgment, because it is inconclusive guesswork, retards the effective elimination of the unworthy. Every breeder of livestock, if he expects to remain in competition with other breeders, must strive constantly to discover the best breeding material at his command, and must eliminate the individuals which are below his standard. Pedigrees, if we except the parents and grandparents, provide so little distinction between good and bad breeding material that it is useless to depend upon them.

What, then, *are* the standards for judging breeding stock, and how dependable are they?

Selection of Stock

The answers to these questions are not to be compressed into a brief work of this nature, and, in all frankness, the answers are not very well known. The experience of a thousand horsemen has not answered, and the research of a few scientists has furnished only crumbs of truth. But, on the basis of numerous investi-

gations, many of them initiated and carried out in offices of the *Blood-Horse* in the last few years, it is possible to make a few generalizations drawn from the consideration of large numbers of instances.

The best evidence of breeding class is, it goes without saying, the actual production of good horses. The racing records of the progeny are the best possible indications of the future racing of future progeny of the same parents.

Before the progeny test can be applied, that is, in appraising young stallions and young mares, the racing class of the individual is the best available indication of the probable racing class of the offspring. This applies as well in females as in males, and for all practical purposes it may be said to apply *especially* to females. It is by far the most important consideration in the selection of breeding stock.

In many cases it will be found that the evidence tending to reveal racing class is inconclusive or lacking altogether. In such cases an estimate may be made from the racing class of the nearest kin (sire, dam, siblings, half-siblings, etc.). An experienced knowledge of conformation may be helpful in cases of this sort. Such estimates, however, should always be made conservatively, and upon the assumption that the indicated probability is less reliable than in the case of actually revealed speed or class. This is simply the method of trial and error, and it must be assumed at the beginning that the incidence of failure will be high, regardless of the standards used in making the original selections.

Young stock selected by this method for breeding purposes should be considered on a probationary status until there is an opportunity to judge them by the performance of their progeny. This is a slow and expensive process and should not be extended further than necessary. There are two chief aids in shortening the probationary period of broodmares:

(1) The second, third, fourth, and fifth foals of a mare have a relatively higher chance of success than the firstling or any of the later foals. Bar-

ring an unusual series of ill fortune, one of the first two or three foals of a mare may be depended on to indicate roughly her potentialities.

(2) There is a correlation between the age of a mare and the class of her offspring, owing presumably to the fact that her vitality decreases with advancing years. The turning point appears to be somewhere around the ages of 12, 13, or 14.

Thus it may be assumed that if a mare has not revealed her speed or racing class (publicly or privately), if she has failed to produce acceptable offspring among her first two or three foals, the odds are very much against her producing acceptable offspring subsequently.

One final generalization: In breeding race horses there are two essential qualities to be considered, speed and stamina. Of these two speed is the commoner, stamina the more rare. In the chance-taking machinery of hereditary processes, stamina (which must include speed) runs the greater risk of being lost, hence the odds are greater against the breeder who sets out to breed a high-class stayer.

The generalizations here set forth must not be regarded as rules. Horse breeding is not to be considered as a game of rules and exceptions. It is rather a game of chance in which the only laws are the laws of probability. The

Chance and Probability

student who is familiar with the almost infinite possibilities in the throw of a handful of dice can visualize the almost infinite possibilities in the mechanism of heredity. Above all, the student who wishes to see clearly the problem of equine heredity should avoid generalizations based upon selected examples, few or many.

Because of the large amount of space that would be required it is not possible to set forth here the *degree* of dependability of the suggested standards of judging breeding stock. Obviously it is low enough that many breeders have failed altogether to recognize it; conversely, it is high enough that many of our most successful breeders have profited by their recognition of it. A

sketchy glance at the probabilities may be afforded by the following rather random details.

The records of 54 prominent stallions, living and dead, were summarized in the *Blood-Horse* of April 4, 1942. Of their 10,257 registered foals of racing age, 62 per cent were winners, 11 per cent were stakes winners, and the average earnings per foal were $6,106. The highest percentage of winners for any one stallion was Ariel's 78 per cent; of stakes winners, *Bull Dog's 18 per cent. The highest average earnings per foal were Fair Play's $10,502 (superseded in 1942 by Equipoise's average).

High-class race mares may be expected to have records approximating the average of the group of stallions just mentioned. They will have about 60 per cent winners, and ordinarily about 10 or 12 per cent of their foals will be stakes winners. This figure is not an arresting one until it is added that mares which failed to reveal racing class well above the average have only 2 or 2.5 per cent of stakes winners among their produce.

An extreme example in American racing of the value of racing class in broodmares is afforded by the Belmont Park Futurity, for years the greatest race for 2-year-olds. Through 1942, 38 per cent of its winners were the progeny of stakes-winning mares—which always constitute less than 5 per cent of the broodmare total.

In closing, the reader is reminded that, in the matter of breeding Thoroughbreds, opinions are rampant and accepted principles are few. The

Work for Tomorrow

hopeful attempts here made toward outlining a few tentative principles may be roundly condemned in some quarters, but we stand by them with confidence until something better is offered. Something better will be offered only when more extensive studies have been made, and it appears reasonable to suppose that some of the students now making the acquaintance of the Thoroughbred eventually will turn their attention to some of the unexplored problems of Thoroughbred breeding, and of horse breeding in general.

Though not exactly a steeplechaser in type, BATTLESHIP is the only American-owned and American-bred winner of the grueling Grand National at Aintree, England, a terrible 4½-mile course over thorn fences, ditches, and water jumps. A son of Man o' War, Battleship was small for his breed, was thought too small for the arduous course.

Sutcliffe Pictures.

16

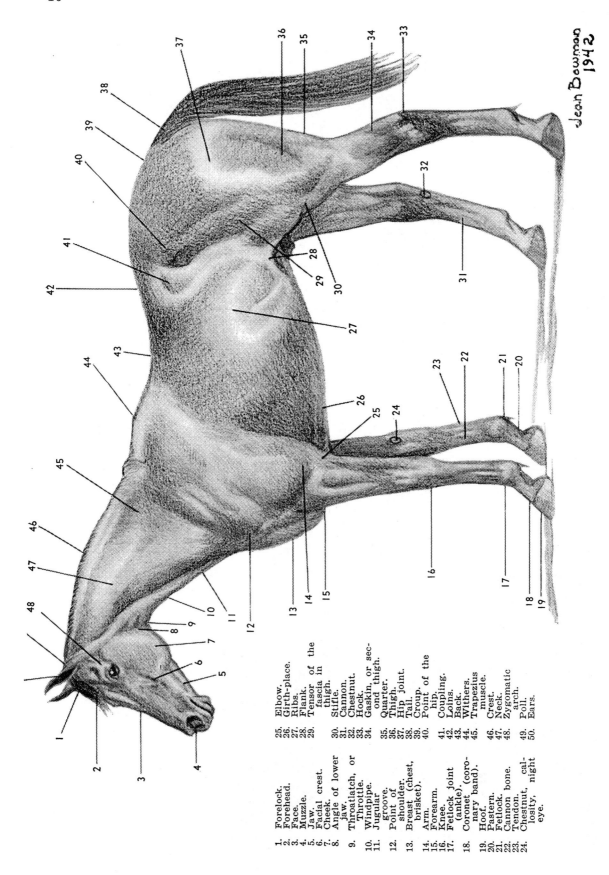

Jean Bowman
1942

1. Forelock.
2. Forehead.
3. Face.
4. Muzzle.
5. Jaw.
6. Facial crest.
7. Cheek.
8. Angle of lower jaw.
9. Throatlatch, or Throttle.
10. Windpipe.
11. Jugular groove.
12. Point of shoulder.
13. Breast (chest, brisket).
14. Arm.
15. Forearm.
16. Knee.
17. Fetlock joint (ankle).
18. Coronet (coronary band).
19. Hoof.
20. Pastern.
21. Fetlock.
22. Cannon bone.
23. Tendon.
24. Chestnut, callosity, night eye.
25. Elbow.
26. Girth-place.
27. Ribs.
28. Flank.
29. Tensor of the fascia in thigh.
30. Stifle.
31. Cannon.
32. Chestnut.
33. Hock.
34. Gaskin, or second thigh.
35. Quarter.
36. Thigh.
37. Hip joint.
38. Tail.
39. Croup.
40. Point of the hip.
41. Coupling.
42. Loins.
43. Back.
44. Withers.
45. Trapezius muscle.
46. Crest.
47. Neck.
48. Zygomatic arch.
49. Poll.
50. Ears.

THE PARTS OF THE HORSE

THE illustration on the opposite page was first published in the *Maryland Horse* of March 1942, and because it was an excellent illustration it was borrowed for reproduction here, with the permission of the artist and of the editor, Humphrey S. Finney.

In anatomy, as in other matters, horsemen disagree, and the terminology accompanying the diagram is not represented as universal usage. In fact, we have changed several of the terms used by the *Maryland Horse* in connection with the same diagram. A few of the terms are quite outside the vocabulary of the horseman; if the average trainer were asked to locate the trapezius muscle of the neck (45) or the zygomatic arch above the eye (48), or to concern himself about the tensor of the fascia in the thigh (29), he would only stare coldly at his tormentor. These terms apparently were included in the numbered series for some special reason, and are repeated here only because they must be accounted for on the illustration.

A few remarks on some of the other names may serve to avoid confusion.

(4) The line points to the nostrils. Muzzle includes nostrils and lips.

(11) Jugular groove: the depression which forms a slight angle with the line of the windpipe.

(12) Point of the shoulder, where the shoulder blade and the arm form a joint.

(13) Brisket, a term rarely used by horsemen, indicates the area extending from the lower part of the neck downward and backward to the girth-place (26).

(14) The arm extends from about the point indicated to the point of the shoulder (12). The point of the elbow is a little higher than indicated by 25.

(15) The forearm, of course, extends from elbow to knee.

(17) To the horseman the fetlock joint is simply the ankle. It corresponds to the human knuckle. The fetlock (21) is the tuft of hair behind the joint. The sesamoid bone is also indicated by 21.

(22) Ordinarily the horseman uses the word cannon to refer to the whole structure between knee and ankle.

(23) When a horse "bows a tendon," it is usually the tendon indicated here which has been strained out of its natural shape. On America's counter-clockwise tracks it is usually the tendon on the near (left) fore leg which gives way.

(26) A horse's girth, as the word is ordinarily used, means the measurement around his body, measured where the saddle-girth fits.

(27) The point indicated is slightly forward of the last ribs.

(28) Flank is a general term for the space between the ribs and the hips. In practice it is most often used to indicate the point here shown, which Mr. Finney calls "the fold of the flank."

(29) Principal function of the "tensor of the fascia" is to move the skin and dislodge flies.

(30) Stifle refers to the joint which corresponds to the human knee. The word is sometimes used loosely to include the area below the joint, toward the hock.

(33) Actually indicated is the point of the hock, or the *os calcis*. The hock is, of course, the entire joint corresponding to the knee in front.

(34) Gaskin includes the leg from the stifle to the hock. Horsemen rarely use the word.

(35) Quarter is a general and not altogether definite term, as used by horsemen. The dictionary calls it, "One leg of a quadruped with the adjacent parts . . . often designating specifically a hindquarter." When a horseman uses the word *quarters* he generally refers to the muscular area of the hips and buttocks. Forequarters are referred to specifically as such.

(37) Occasionally one finds the point numbered 40 called the hip joint, but there is no movable joint at 40.

(41) The point designated here is the depression between the hindmost ribs and the point of the hip. Coupling refers more specifically to that part of the spinal column between the last ribs and the pelvis. Mr. Finney describes 41 as "coupling—or hunger hollow."

(42) The loins extend across the back.

(43) The saddle-place is indicated here. The back extends from the withers to the point of the croup (highest part of the hindquarters), which is not numbered in the diagram.

A few general terms have been omitted in the above discussion. *Forehand* refers to that part of the animal in front of the saddle. The *shoulder* is the area of the shoulder blade, which extends from the withers (44) to the point of the shoulder (12). *Barrel* is the body of the horse between the shoulders and the flanks. The *near* side of the horse is the side from which he is mounted, that is, the left; the *off* side is the right.

Width between the eyes, firm molding of mouth and nostrils, well placed ears, flat profile, intelligent eyes, and a general air of strength and poise are the ideal attributes of the Thoroughbred head. This is MAN O' WAR.

Brownie Leach.

CONFORMATION: The Principles by Which Horsemen Attempt to Distinguish Between Good Performers and Others—With Questionable Success.

THE everlasting emphasis on speed as the primary requirement in the Thoroughbred necessarily has specialized the breed and endowed it with characteristics, inward and outward, which set it apart from other types of horses. It has fined down and hardened the skeletal structure, especially in the extremities; it has developed muscles whose strength approaches, and sometimes exceeds, the maximum strain that can be borne by the joints, bones, and tendons; it has demanded such excellence of performance from all parts of the body that the breed itself demands special attention in the matter of nutrition and care, as long as the Thoroughbred is called upon to carry out its hereditary function of racing in competition against its peers. The emphasis on speed has changed also the psychological as well as physical nature of the animal. It

Differences from Other Breeds

has made him, if not more intelligent, more courageous than other horses; more intolerant of opposition, but, once his confidence has been gained and his lessons taught, more efficient in the performance of utility tasks which lie within his physical compass; more determined to finish the

job assigned him, regardless of the odds. The unreasoning courage by which a race horse with three good legs and one broken beyond repair will go on to victory in a race sets him apart from horses in general as definitely as his lean frame and his fine skin. It is this temperament which causes Thoroughbred horsemen to refer to non-Thoroughbreds as cold-blooded horses. It is this complete courage which sparks the improvement wrought upon utility horses by an admixture of Thoroughbred blood.

Except for these differences, of speed and its physical requirements on the one hand, and of "hot" temperament, or all-out courage, on the other, the standards for judging the individual Thoroughbred are very much the same as for judging horses in general. Generally speaking, the great majority of characteristics which would be charged up as faults against any other breed are also faults with the Thoroughbred, and no great modification of accepted principles will be necessary. Hence no exhaustive cataloguing of good and bad points of horses in general is attempted here.

As a matter of fact, the records of racing confute the supposition that even the ablest of Thoroughbred horsemen can set down "rules" of judging conformation and individuality. Horses being what they are, they would not read the rules, anyway.

One of the oldest axioms of the race track is, "They run in all shapes and sizes." This is true to the extent of creating no end of confusion among those who would specify the *best* shapes and sizes. There is a tremendous range in size among good horses, roughly from about 14 hands 2 inches to 17 hands, and from 700 pounds to about twice that weight. And as to shape, there can be found good horses to argue against the importance of even the most universally accepted "faults," such as ewe necks, flat withers, straight shoulders, calf knees, straight pasterns, club feet, long backs, goose rumps, sickle hocks, and so on. The great majority of good Thoroughbreds will fall within a range of five inches in height, from 15:1 to 16:2 and within a range of 250 pounds (under training conditions), from 000 to 1,150. The great majority of the good ones will be found comparatively free of those characteristics which are most confidently set down as faults. But the occurrence among the good ones of the undersized, the oversized, and the faulty is frequent enough to dissuade most horsemen from being positive about what it takes to make a good horse.

All Shapes and Sizes

A fine knowledge of conformation, consequently, is no infallible guide in estimating horses, at least partly because such important matters as lung capacity, digestive ability, the circulation of the blood, and even intelligence and disposition, are not subject to immediate appraisal through inspection. Furthermore, there is what horsemen call "heart"—the will and determination to win— and this is measurable only in the stress of actual competition. The Australian horse Carbine, for example, ordinarily good-tempered and cheerful to the point of mischievousness, is reputed always to have pulled up in a terrific temper when he was beaten, and would sometimes try to bite anyone who came in his reach. And sometimes others, whose names never become famous, will

work six furlongs against the watch in 1:12, and be beaten in slower time.

Despite this, the study of conformation is valuable, first, in estimating the chances of a horse to stand intensive training without breaking down—as a gauge of soundness, in other words— and, second, in forming an estimate of the physical efficiency of the racing mechanism as it appears to the eye. Here, as elsewhere, we deal in probabilities, not in rules and exceptions, and the student may be assured that a sound knowledge of conformation does make the probabilities more favorable.

The following comments on conformation are not, of course, to be regarded as fixed, indisputable principles. Opinions differ, and a horseman who has trained a very good horse of one type is likely to be looking for that type again, regardless of whether it seems a more successful type than others generally. Similarly, when a horse proves durable and useful, despite a specific physical defect, the trainer of that horse will tend to minimize that defect in other horses. But viewing the horse as a purely physical mechanism, of so much power, with levers and pulleys over which to exert it, the subjoined comments will perhaps serve until experience and study have improved upon them. The ordinary principles of physics apply, and the greatest force, exerted with the greatest economy of effort, produces the fastest horse.

No horseman wants a head "like a bull fiddle" on a horse, but the Thoroughbred horseman is especially careful, in choosing an animal, to see that the head is in proportion to the remainder, for the head and neck are very important in maintaining balance, which is all-important in

Dish face, too short neck, low withers, straight shoulder, calf-knees, upright pastern, sickle hocks, goose rump.

running at top speed or in clearing a steeplechase jump. The successful trainers with the longest experience are almost unanimous in insisting upon what they call an "intelligent" head. One principal clue to this supposed intelligence is the broad space between the eyes, another, the eye itself, which, in the words of a commentator of nearly a century ago, "should be kindly, strong, bold, and fiery, yet gentle looking." Small eyes (which horsemen call "pig eyes") are avoided, and some horsemen can make out quite a case against a horse which shows an excessive amount of white around the edges.

Head

Lop ears take away greatly from the beauty of the horse, but whether they have any connection

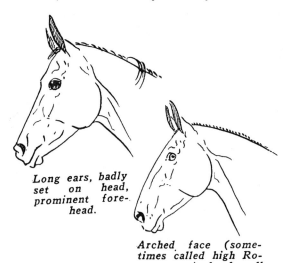

Long ears, badly set on head, prominent forehead.

Arched face (sometimes called high Roman nose), head well set on short, thick neck.

with speed is a subject to leave open for debate. The profile generally preferred is straight. Most horsemen abhor the convex line, or "Roman nose," believing it a sign of temper or intractability. Some of them object to a concavity below the eyes—the effect commonly called "dish-face"—but others accept this merely as a pleasant outward sign of high breeding, since it recalls handsome, delicately beautiful Arabian ancestry. At all events, they prefer a moderately tapered muzzle with sensitive, large nostrils, fine, tight lips, divided well back. The jowl, they are especially insistent, should be deep, as viewed from the side, and wide-angled, as felt from below, to allow great room for the air passage at the throttle. Occasionally a horse is seen whose head is set on at such a sharp angle as to suggest that when the pressure of the rein is on his mouth the resulting pressure on the throttle might inhibit to some extent the extreme activity of the breathing apparatus which is essential to high-speed efforts.

In the race horse the head should be comparatively low. If it is placed on a fairly upright neck, it cannot serve as well for the important function of a balance-pole, a very necessary item when the horse is taking the tremendous leaps which constitute the running gait, and as a result the gait will be "higher," less even, and more wasteful of energy. For the same reason the neck which bears it should be moderately long, in comparison with other breeds, and lighter, but not to the point of

Neck

weakness. It should be arched slightly, not heavily crested (while in training), nor laden anywhere with unnecessary muscle.

The withers should be high, firm, moderately thin (never "fat"), and clearly defined. Functionally, the withers represent a prolongation of the processes of the vertebrae, and it is to these bones that the muscles running to the shoulder are attached. Since the amount of contraction possible in a muscle is proportioned to the muscle's length, it is obvious that high withers, adding to the length of these muscles, are desirable.

Withers

The shoulder should be sloped, the more the better, as a horse's reach—that is, the angle at which he can project his fore legs to the front—depends largely on this factor. For the same reason a "loaded" shoulder—one surrounded by too much flesh, or "lumber," particularly in front—is undesirable. The great English horse St. Simon was a particular example of good shoulders. His stud groom, John Huby, said of him:

Shoulder

His shoulder was a study. So obliquely was it placed that it appeared to extend far into his back, making the latter look shorter—and as a matter of fact it was shorter—than any horse's back I have ever seen. . . . there is little wonder that he showed such marvelous liberty of action.

The lower end of the shoulder blade, where it forms a joint with the humerus, or arm, is denoted as the point of the shoulder. The humerus extends backward and downward to the elbow where it joins the bones of the forearm. Although it gets less attention than the shoulder blade because it is more overlaid with muscle, its length and position are no less important. It will be seen at a glance that the longer the humerus, and the greater the angle it makes with the scapula, or shoulder blade, the

Arm and Forearm

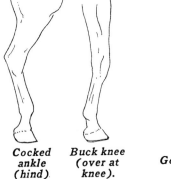

Cocked ankle (hind). *Buck knee (over at knee).* *Good fore leg.*

longer the muscles will be which operate these bones; and the more nearly the humerus approaches the perpendicular, the more freely the forearm can be thrown forward in a long, easy stride. In this connection it might be pointed out that the point of the shoulder should not be extremely prominent, a condition which would imply a lessening of the angle between the scapula and the humerus.

At the elbow, where the forearm joins the humerus, or upper arm, there should be a wide expanse of muscle attachments, with strong muscles tapering toward the knee. A lightly muscled forearm does not prevent a horse from being a good racer, provided the bones are well placed in this area, but a strong forearm provides by far the better gamble, since it includes all the muscles which act upon the lower part of the leg— the most constantly and heavily punished portion of the race horse's anatomy.

Possibly the most important area for inspection in judging is the fore leg. Trotters frequently develop trouble behind, but the Thoroughbred, carrying weight more or less amidships, punishes his fore legs more than any other part of his body, and it is here that **Fore Leg** most of his unsoundness develops, aside from accidental injury or general ill health. If it is remembered that a racing horse, traveling at a speed which at times exceeds 40 miles an hour, lands with an average weight of about a half-ton, and that it is the slender columns of the fore legs which take the shock, it is easy to see why these are heir to trouble.

As viewed from the side, the fore leg should be a straight column down to the fetlock joint, or ankle, as horsemen almost invariably call it (though it isn't an ankle at all, as compared with human anatomy, but rather a knuckle). If there is a slight angle at the knee, it should be bent for-

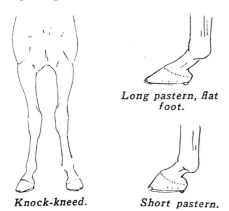

Long pastern, flat foot.

Knock-kneed.   *Short pastern.*

ward rather than back. If the upper and lower portions of the leg are inclined slightly forward at the knee, the horse is said to be "over at the knees," or "buck-kneed." While this condition represents no improvement over the normal straight line, it is not a fault, unless extreme. Galopin and his son St. Simon, two of the greatest race horses and sires in England during the last century, and in America the good sprinter *Voter and the Kentucky Derby winners Bubbling Over and his son Burgoo King are examples of buck-kneed horses. But if the horse is "calf-kneed," with a slight angle pointing backward at the knee, he has a very serious fault and must be extra good elsewhere to be worth considering, since this condition puts an extraordinary strain upon tendons and ligaments.

The knee, viewed from the side, should be flat and smooth on the front surface, with a well defined projection at the rear, where the tendons pass. Ridged or "baggy" knees, while they sometimes go with good horses, are danger signs, especially if the skin over the knee is loose. The **Knee and Cannon** knee joint should taper into the full width of the cannon; if there is an abrupt narrowing, below which the cannon widens again, the horse is said to be "tied in," and the condition prevents the tendon from acting in a straight

line and furnishes a considerable hazard to the ligament which binds the tendon at this point. From the front, the knee should appear large and "tight." A small knee will not have sufficient space for the attachment of tendons and ligaments.

The cannon, from knee to ankle, should be short and comparatively flat. The bone wants to be in keeping with the size of the horse, since a fine bone will not carry an oversized load without trouble and a heavy bone will impede the progress of a light horse. The tendons which lie behind the bone should be set out distinctly, as indicated by the contour of the skin, and the farther back they lie and the straighter they run from the back of the knee to the fetlock joint the more efficiently they will operate.

The fetlock joint, or ankle, is the seat of many troubles, but it takes a very practiced eye to distinguish here between good and bad. It needs to **Ankle and Pastern** be large for the attachment of ligaments and tendons, but should not be so large, or the contour of the bones so rounded off and obscured, as to suggest softness. A prominence at the inside rear "corner" suggests sesamoiditis, or inflammation at the sesamoid bone. But the neophyte should not trust his suspicions regarding ankles; better ask a veterinarian.

The pastern should make an angle of a little less than 45 degrees with the perpendicular when the horse is standing firmly on all four legs. It is the pastern which takes up a good deal of the shock of landing, and it is important that it be strong and springy. Short, stubby pasterns are not springy enough; long ones are too weak to hold the fetlock joint off the ground. Straight, or upright, pasterns, when the angle with the cannon bone is larger than normal, very often cause unsoundness. Horses with too straight pasterns frequently run fast; they usually do not run far or last long.

Such obvious troubles as ringbone or sidebone, both exostoses, or bony growths, on the pastern, are not considered here. Though not very important in work horses, they frequently mar the usefulness of Thoroughbreds. Though occasionally found on yearlings, they usually appear later, either as the result of a blow, or from injuries incidental to fast work. Splints are also bony growths, usually appearing on the cannons fairly well up to the knee and on the inside of the leg. If not too close to the joint, or far enough back to involve a tendon, splints are seldom serious.

The hoof should be large, and well open at the heel. Small feet, or contracted feet (which form an oval slightly broken at the back) are liabilities. **Foot** Small feet may be considered to have grown that way in the natural course of events. Contracted feet, which cause trouble because they create pressure on the delicate inner mechanism, are usually

Good foot and contracted foot.

the result of disease or accident or lack of proper care. Shelly feet, which frequently break off or crack around the toes, are a source of trouble and do not hold the shoe as firmly as they should. Many horsemen believe a white hoof is weaker than a dark-colored one. Irregularities in the surface of the hoof do not necessarily mean that the wall is weak. The front of the hoof, as seen from the side of the horse, should continue the line of the front of the pastern, or nearly so.

The assembly of the fore legs should always be inspected from in front of the horse. The "fork" of the fore legs should be in proportion to the width of the body, and if it varies greatly from the normal a wide fork is perhaps prefer-

Front View able to a narrow one; either may be responsible for an irregularity in gait. Occasionally there will be found a horse so narrow-chested that the forearms are barely separated. A few horsemen insist that a wide fork indicates a sprinter; but a wide fork goes properly with a wide body.

The line of the fore leg as seen from the front should be as nearly plumb as possible, with no

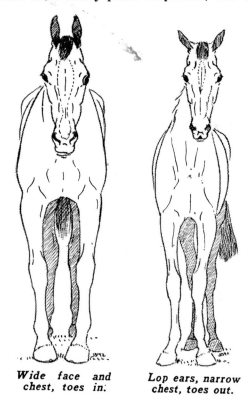

Wide face and chest, toes in.

Lop ears, narrow chest, toes out.

bending in or out at the knee or below the ankle. It is obvious that a knock-kneed horse, or one whose toes turn in or out, cannot operate as efficiently as one whose system of levers and pulleys offers no chance of waste motion. The impression gained by looking at the horse while standing should be checked further by watching him at the walk. The feet should be pointed in the direction in which he is moving and should move through each stride in an almost straight line. If the feet definitely turn in or out, let the eye follow up the leg to determine whether the variation from normal begins at the coronet, the ankle, the knee, or the elbow; ordinarily, the higher up the twisting from normal appears, the more certainly it may be set down as a fault. In the matter of demanding perfection of the fore legs of a race horse, however, one should be very

cautious indeed; so few of them will be found to meet any set of specifications that one must nearly always choose among so-called faults and hope that the ones accepted will prove to be the least consequential.

The line of the back should curve evenly downward from the withers, and just back of the saddle begin a much more gradual ascent to the

Body croup. If the back arches up badly at the loins, the horse is said to be "roach-backed" or "hog-backed," and this is not a usual characteristic of good horses. The barrel should be roomy, with the ribs well sprung (a herring-ribbed, or slab-sided, horse is one whose ribs drop downward sharply from the spine), and the depth from saddle to chest—most easily measured as girth—is some indication of heart and lung room.

The estimate of a race horse's chest, however, ought to be made on a three-dimensional basis, and since it is such an important matter, it is well to give a little extra attention to the means of making the estimate. Roughly, the chest occupies the section bounded by the neck and breast in front, the spine above, the breastbone below, and the diaphragm behind. The muscular diaphragm, which extends across the body, dividing the chest from the abdominal cavity, slants forward and downward, from the kidneys, behind the saddle, to a point on the belly just behind the girth. Thus spaciousness and efficiency of the lungs can be approximated from outward indications, such as the depth of the body through the girth, the width of the body as seen from in front, and the shape as seen from the front. The general shape of a cross-section through the chest should be rather more of an ellipse and less of a circle than in breeds of less strenuous functions, since the ellipse can be expanded at the sides to increase the capacity for drawing in air, whereas if the chest is more of a circle in the first place it has less chance of adequate expansion.

Most of the foregoing, except for the remarks concerning the muscling around the shoulder, arm, and forearm, has to do with the efficiency of the horse as a racing mechanism. When we come to the hindquarters we are considering the main source of power, which lies in the great muscles there. The important area is the tri-

Hind-quarters angle formed by the hip bone (from the point of the hip backward and slightly downward toward the point of the buttock) and the thigh bone, or femur, which extends from the hip joint to the stifle joint. The mechanism here roughly parallels that of the shoulder blade and the humerus, and here, as in front, a long femur and a comparatively wide angle are to be looked for. The length of the bone indicates to some extent the space for the attachment of strong muscles, the size of the angle determines the length of the muscles. The large angle provides longer muscles and allows a more complete extension of the joint, the result being a longer, more powerful stride.

The strong musculature of the hip and thigh should be continued into the gaskin, whose muscles operate the lower part of the leg. If the outline of the gaskin cuts in sharply at the rear below the haunch, the horse is said to be cat-hammed, and a fault is set down against him. A broad gaskin goes with a long os calcis (point of the hock), which means a long lever over which the tendon can operate. The hock should be set low—length from hip to hock is a frequent point of commendation—and it should be large. In general, the more nearly straight the hind leg is (the larger the angle at the hock) the better the horseman will like it, since a hind leg that appears too straight is an extreme rarity. If the angle here is much narrower than normal the leg cannot be extended fully, and part of its power will be lost. If the curve is very sweeping the horse is said to be sickle-hocked, a figure of speech which describes the fault aptly enough. The crooked hind leg is more apt to develop a curb, a straining or inflammation of the ligament which binds the tendon to the hind cannon a short distance below the point of the hock. If the straight line along the back of the cannon is broken by a slight outward bulge, easily seen from the side, the horse has a curb, which may or may not affect his running.

Standing directly behind the horse may reveal faults not otherwise easily discovered. If the

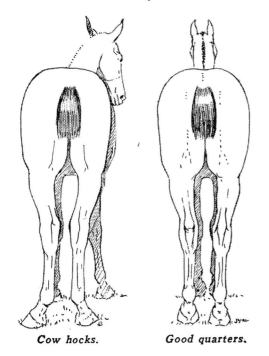

Cow hocks.   Good quarters.

body is too narrow in proportion to height, if it slopes away too sharply from the croup, or if the muscles are not well enough let down from the haunches, the animal is weak in a most important part of his anatomy. The hocks, as seen from the rear, should point almost straight back; if they turn definitely inward the horse is said to be cow-hocked, and he is definitely the worse for it.

All these details are more or less important—in what rank they have importance it would take a bold horseman to declare. But they still need to be supplemented by general considerations of type, substance, symmetry, stance, action, quality, and disposition. Most of the knowledge here available is knowledge applicable to many breeds, the variations necessary for the Thoroughbred being more or less obvious.

General As a matter of fact there is a very great range within the Thoroughbred breed itself. It takes an experienced eye to see where substance, for instance, is adequate between the light-waisted, "one-gutted" specimen on the one hand and the beefy sort on the other; to judge whether quality (thin skin, fine hair,

smooth "finish") is an indication of true Thoroughbred characteristics or is simply a deluding prettiness; or to decide between easy-going docility and rip-roaring assertiveness.

Very little has been said about muscle, and perhaps very little can be said. A lightly muscled horse is at an obvious disadvantage and the condition is easily recognized. Generally speaking, long flat muscles are to be preferred to short bunchy ones. Also generally speaking, the driving power is in the hindquarters, and these should be particularly well muscled, and wide

Muscles as viewed from behind. It is quite possible for a horse to be too heavily muscled, and to be simply strong rather than fast. Sprinters are characteristically more heavily muscled than stayers—that is, their muscles appear to be laid on more heavily, and thick rather than long. But nearly all of these are generalizations which are not to be relied upon too heavily. Eliminating individuals which have something basically wrong with them, muscle can be developed by exercise and good food, whereas the structure of bone and tendon is much less easily modified. Of course a yearling which is stunted has passed much of his normal growing period, and the best of handling is likely to fail to bring him to proper development. However, assuming reasonable size and good health in a young horse, bone structure is a more reliable guide to conformation than musculature.

In this connection it seems fitting to challenge a certain race track axiom, "A long horse for a long race." The truth of this matter seems to be diametrically opposite to the old saw. The horse which is long-bodied in proportion to his height is almost invariably a sprinter; the horse which is tall in proportion to his body length, while he may be a good sprinter, is likely to gain greater success at the longer distances. This generalization is based upon the study of

Long Horses vs. Tall numerous pictures of good horses, and the exceptions found were comparatively rare. The length measurements were taken from the point where the neck joins the brisket, back to the point of the buttocks, or a perpendicular line dropped from that point. Ordinarily this measurement is roughly the same as the height of the horse; if it is definitely longer, the staying power of that individual may be presumed to be slight. The explanation here seems easy enough. The short-legged horse pushes himself along by the extravagant use of powerful muscles. The legs of the short-bodied horse are longer pendulums and their oscillations will be a trifle more deliberate, using a little less energy with each stride, saving a little more energy for the closing furlongs of the longer race.

Finally, in the matter of "judging" the conformation of a prospective race horse, it must be remembered always that it is the judge, rather than the horse, who is on trial. The speed of the horse is not likely to be affected in the least by the opinion of a man who has walked around him once or twice. Hence it is suggested that anyone who wishes to study Thoroughbred conformation make it a practice to keep records of his observations and predictions and check them against the records of actual racing.

In the office of the *Blood-Horse* are notes on the conformation of several thousand Thoroughbreds, made mostly when the horses were yearlings. The notes are made on 5x8" cards like the illustration on the inside back cover. Departures from normal, whether for better or for worse,

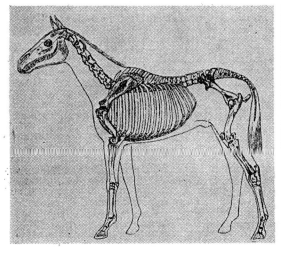

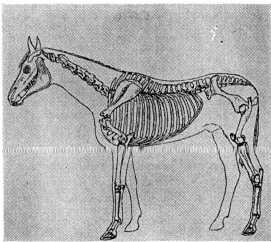

PERSIMMON   GLEN STIRLING

The above illustrations are taken from Points of a Racehorse (1903), *by Maj. Gen. Sir John Hills, who used them to illustrate the importance of the position and relative length of the scapula (shoulder blade) and humerus (upper arm). On the left is the first-class racer and noted sire Persimmon, on the right the third-rate Glen Stirling. In the case of Persimmon note the greater angle between scapula and humerus, the more upright position and greater relative length of the humerus. (From drawings made in the Royal Veterinary University.)*

can be easily indicated on the outlined figures. Racing performances and later inspections can be added to the record. Except for those privileged to have a long and intimate acquaintance with horses, this is perhaps the most effective way of learning what is important in the way of conformation. Memory has a way of playing tricks; it is much easier to forget the case in which we were wrong than the one in which we were right.

There is no "point system" for scoring Thoroughbreds, nor is one likely to be devised. The card used by the *Blood-Horse* is rather a record of details necessary for reporting and for study later. If the observer wishes, he can indicate his guesses as to probable class and distance preference on the scale indicated by the broken lines in the lower left-hand corner, but this is strictly an exercise in harmless mental betting.

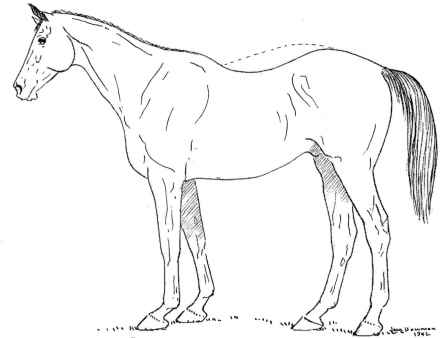

Lop ears, sway back (roach back shown dotted line), curby hocks, long pasterns.

CARE AND USES: A Few Precautionary Reminders on Handling the Thoroughbred, Plus Notes on the Utility of Thoroughbred Blood.

The following section was contributed by Humphrey S. Finney, editor of the Maryland Horse *and field secretary of the Maryland Horse Breeders' Association. It was also through the kindness of the* Maryland Horse *that the illustrations in the chapter on conformation were made available.*

THERE are not many differences between the accepted mode of raising the Thoroughbred and the procedure followed on most farms where horses of other kinds are raised, the same rules of sound animal husbandry applying to all. But some of the differences are important, and the average farmer, used to raising farm stock, should reconsider some of his methods before he attempts the breeding of Thoroughbreds.

It is common for farm stock to run out most of the grazing season, depending entirely on pasture for sustenance. The Thoroughbred mare, even when in foal, can get along very well on good pasture, but it should be *good* pasture, not what passes for pasture on many farms.

The care of the Thoroughbred foal commences on the day the mare is bred for the first time. A word here about the trials of the mare. While draft mares will usually come in season regularly every 21 days or thereabouts, the Thoroughbred mare may have a cycle varying from 14 to 28 days, though usually from 18 to 21 days. Consequently it is highly important that *all* mares that have been bred be tried at least twice a week, and preferably every other day, throughout the breeding season, commencing two weeks after service.

There are many, unfamiliar with blooded stock, who think that the Thoroughbred is a nervous, ratty beast. Nothing is further from the truth. The Thoroughbred mare, as a rule, is a gentle animal, though it must be remembered that, if she is mean, she may be a hellion, for it is the nature of the beast to make a thorough job of whatever it undertakes.

The Thoroughbred mare is likely to be a quicker-acting and -thinking animal than the farmer-breeder is used to. It is highly important that she be handled with quiet consideration, for shouting and yelling at her may produce a good deal worse results than if the same treatment were accorded a cold-blooded mare. Thoroughbreds can be tied in standing stalls, but they should be made used to it carefully, as most likely it will be a new experience for the majority of them. Thoroughbred mares will do very well

Bert Clark Thayer.

The most popular horse of the late 'thirties was SEABISCUIT, grandson of Man o' War. By winning his last start, the Santa Anita Handicap of 1940, he became the world's leading money winner, a distinction that lasted two years.

running out all winter, provided they have plenty to eat and a dry wind-breaking shed to go into when they feel like it.

The Thoroughbred mare at foaling time is no different from the cold-blooded mare, except that she may make heavier weather of it, if in trouble, and fight harder for her existence if things go wrong. The blooded foal is usually a quicker, handier thing than the cold-blooded one. Many foals are lost on farms from neglect of the simple matter of caring for the navel cord at birth, with attendant joint-ill, or navel-ill, through infection.

The feet of the Thoroughbred should be watched and trimmed monthly, a more important matter with him than with other breeds. He can be raised with his mother as the rest of them are, but if his dam is taken out to work for part of the day, as are many draft mares, the Thoroughbred foal is more likely to fret and injure himself. Hence he should have company of some sort if possible. When weaned the Thoroughbred foal should by all means be kept up for a few days, for he is likely to "run his head off" if turned out too soon, much more so than the cold-blood.

The Thoroughbred is full of fire and courage by nature. He can easily be led, but he is hard to drive. Obedience will come through training and kindness, but rarely through force. If you want to handle him with success, get him used to the halter, to leading, standing tied, backing up, having all his feet picked up, and to loading and shipping about also, if possible, when he is very young—the younger the better. If you try to halter-break and to handle a Thoroughbred for the first time when he is a big yearling, you are simply asking for trouble.

The whole matter of raising the Thoroughbred, or any other livestock for that matter, is one of common horse sense. Just stop to consider what you are doing, and why, and you'll get along all right.

The Thoroughbred, though his chief aim and object in life is the winning of races and the production of more winners, has numerous other fields of endeavor for which he has superb qualifications. His prowess in the hunting field, at polo, in the show ring, or as a plain hack is well known. In these fields the clean-bred horse is supreme, though the half-bred may do as well or almost as well in some cases.

The writer once mated a big, upstanding Thoroughbred stallion to some well-bred Percheron mares and thereby bred some really outstanding medium-weight farm horses that would stand more heat and grief than any teams about the place. We have seen some very useful horses bred the reverse way. Some breeders have used a Thoroughbred-Percheron cross as the basis of successful hunter-breeding operations; the results here are usually best in the second cross, where a Thoroughbred sire is used on the half-bred stock.

J. A. Estes.

A great stayer was Greentree Stable's TWENTY GRAND, whose Kentucky Derby record lasted until Whirlaway's time. Foaled in 1928, Twenty Grand was one of the great crop of foals which included Equipoise, Mate, Jamestown, and others. The picture was made in May of his 4-year-old year.

Thoroughbred mares bred to good jacks have produced many excellent mules, particularly suitable to light quick work. Thoroughbred mares themselves have been worked successfully on many farms. They have the courage and tireless ability to do a day's work in good style, if not put to too heavy labor. We have used a hitch of three or four barren mares to a harrow on a Thoroughbred breeding farm. It is important, however, that plenty of care be taken in breaking them to work, for the Thoroughbred mare is a quick thinker and a quick mover. A quiet, careful, experienced teamster is indicated here.

The Thoroughbred mare, when crossed with the Cleveland Bay stallion, has produced some good heavyweight hunters, better, as a rule, than with the reverse of the cross. The second cross of Thoroughbred sire is likely to produce a superior animal. It is essential here that the mare used be a mare of style and quality, if a really saleable product is to be developed. Some of the top halfbred hunters in Virginia carry Cleveland Bay blood. A Thoroughbred-Suffolk cross has been tried with varying results. Some big hunters have been produced in that fashion.

The best results in half-bred breeding have resulted from the use of the Thoroughbred sire for generations on grade mares. Some of the western ranches that have been in the business for many years have as fine a lot of cow horses as one would wish to see—big, strong, tough horses, up to weight, and with speed and durability—that are very nearly clean-bred animals. The cow country comes nearer proving the right blood to use than anywhere else, for there the old law of the survival of the fittest gets more play, and the non-producing sires and dams are soon weeded out.

(Editor's note: Melville H. Haskell's remarks on the problem of raising quarter horses and cow horses on the western ranges are appropriate here. Quoted from the *Blood-Horse* of September 12, 1942: "As far as I am concerned, the answer is simple. Start with a band of good quarter mares of the deep-bodied, easy-keeping type that were raised on the range and know how to rustle for a living and that give milk like a Jersey. Cull poor keepers or mares that do not raise big healthy foals without help. Use on these mares the best Thoroughbred sire that you can buy, of as near the type you want as you can find. Cull the ones that can't make a living or are faulty. On the second generation fillies you may have to use a half-bred quarter horse type stallion, but be sure that he has good blood and breeds true. You will produce economically in this way a very useful type of horse, hardy, handy, quick—a horse that will appeal to the old fashioned cowman and the lover of the Thoroughbred alike.")

Whatever use the Thoroughbred is put to, he or she must be a decent sort of animal to make good at it. All of us know that there are too many weedy, light-boned, ewe-necked beasts that never should be bred from; yet, simply because they have a certificate, they are used to produce something that, in the end, nine times out of ten, will discredit the breed. Whatever the intent of the breeder seeking to use Thoroughbred blood, let him use the same rigid rules of selection that he, in all likelihood, applies to his beef or dairy herd, or his draft stock. A pedigree does not make a Thoroughbred a good horse if nature has not done her part in the physical makeup of the animal.

BOOKS AND REFERENCES: Suggestions for the Further and More Specialized Study of the Thoroughbred.

THE literature from which the beginner may learn the elementary principles and background of Thoroughbred breeding and racing is not widely distributed, nor is it readily available in inexpensive form. If it were, this pamphlet would not have been necessary. But the following notes may be of assistance to those who wish to pursue the subject further.

A basic statistical work of the American Turf is the *American Racing Manual,* published annually by *Daily Racing Form* (441 Plymouth Court, Chicago, Ill.), and available at $3 a copy if bound in paper, or $3.50 if bound in boards. It furnishes the most complete statistical breakdown of each year's racing and has numerous compilations based upon the racing of earlier years. It is virtually the only low-priced comprehensive record of each year's racing.

The *American Stud Book,* issued every four years, costs $25 a copy. The monthly chart books (showing details of all races run) sell at $2.00 for each monthly volume. The *Blood-Horse* publishes *Thoroughbred Sires and Dams,* an annual volume which furnishes the only comprehensive analysis of racing results from the point of view of the breeder concerned with evaluating breeding stock; because the distribution is small and the work is enormous, the prices of these volumes vary from $17.50 upwards. The *Blood-Horse* also publishes a loose-leaf *Stallion Register* showing five-cross pedigrees and other information on approximately 200 stallions; the price is $10. *American Race Horses,* an annual series on famous horses, written by a noted authority, John L. Hervey, sells for $7.50. These items are only rarely found in school libraries.

One of the most valuable and least expensive references on the subject is entitled *A Quarter-Century of American Racing.* It was issued in August, 1941, when the *Blood-Horse* celebrated its twenty-fifth anniversary, and extra copies are available at 50 cents each, postage included. It includes a running account of the best racing since 1916, an extended article on pedigrees and breeding, tabulated pedigrees of 118 outstanding horses, and much other material. It is the best inexpensive volume on the recent history of racing and the Thoroughbred in America.

The *Blood-Horse* publishes at the end of each year a supplement giving tabulated pedigrees of all stakes winners of the year, together with much other valuable information having to do with the year's best horses. These supplements are sent free to subscribers of the *Blood-Horse,* and extra copies are available at 25 cents each. Back numbers since and including 1936 are obtainable.

The best text available on the care and management of Thoroughbreds and other light breeds is Col. John F. Wall's *A Horseman's Handbook on Practical Breeding,* the latest revision of which is priced at $4. Address American Remount Association, 809 Otis Building, 810 18th St., Washington, D. C. *A Stud Farm Diary,* by Humphrey S. Finney, published at $1 after running serially in the *Blood-Horse,* is now out of print.

Books on training horses for racing are in demand. *Race Horse Training,* an excellent volume by Robert W. Collins, ran serially in the

28

Blood-Horse and was published in book form, but the edition was quickly sold out. *Training for Fun—and Profit Maybe,* a well organized discussion by Keene Daingerfield, Jr., was published serially in the *Thoroughbred Record* (Lexington, Ky.) and has just been published in book form, at $3.50 a copy.

There is no book which discusses adequately the various problems of genetics, matings, bloodlines, and principles of breeding. Although numerous books on such matters have been published, most of them concern such unverifiable theories as the Bruce Lowe Figure Guide and the Vuillier dosage system, and few of them have practical value. Numerous studies on these problems, based upon research comparing good horses with the "average of the breed," have been published in the *Blood-Horse.* A most interesting series of articles on noted ancestors, entitled *Names in Pedigrees,* written by Joe H. Palmer, was published serially in the *Blood-Horse* and is available in book form, at $3 a copy. An excellent popularized version of the science of genetics, with special application to farm products (plants and animals), will be found in the 1936 *Yearbook of Agriculture,* issued by the United States Department of Agriculture. The section having to do with horses, however, is less comprehensive than most of the others, largely because information in this field was available to a lesser degree.

For detailed study of the art of horsemanship, including studies of conformation, gaits, training for riding, and so on, one of the best books is *Points of the Horse,* by Capt. M. H. Hayes, which may occasionally be found through a second-hand dealer. It does not concern itself primarily with Thoroughbreds.

For the study of anatomy and diseases, the United States Department of Agriculture's *Diseases of the Horse,* last revised in 1923, is excellent. It may be purchased for $1 or obtained through a senator or congressman. The Department of Agriculture also has bulletins on judging horses and on the care of farm animals, and a very important bulletin on horse parasites, available at nominal prices.

Among periodicals devoted to the Thoroughbred, the *Blood-Horse,* published weekly at Lexington, Ky., by the American Thoroughbred Breeders Association, offers a running account of racing and breeding developments in North America and abroad, with numerous articles of a general nature and with special attention to the interests of breeders. The *Thoroughbred Record* is also published weekly at Lexington. Several state associations of breeders have publications, including the *Maryland Horse* and the *Ohio Horse,* which "cover" not only Thoroughbreds but other breeds, and the *Thoroughbred* (California). The American Remount Association, with headquarters in Washington, D. C., publishes an interesting bi-monthly magazine, *The Horse.* The *Chronicle,* published at Middleburg, Va., is a weekly newspaper devoted largely to the interests of hunters and show-ring enthusiasts. Addressed largely to bettors, but including numerous interesting articles on various phases and personalities of the Turf, is the *Turf and Sport Digest,* published monthly in Baltimore and distributed mostly through newsstand sales. The most complete coverage of the Turf, of course, is provided by *Daily Racing Form,* an extraordinary newspaper, which sells at 25 cents a copy and is more or less indispensable to those who make bets on the races.

The *Blood-Horse* has small reprints available of articles on the Bruce Lowe Figure Guide, the registration of Thoroughbreds, and "Are Pedigrees Important?", a study by Dr. Dewey G. Steele, geneticist, University of Kentucky.

The public libraries of the country have comparatively little material for reference on the Thoroughbred, but most of the larger ones have a few books or periodicals. The most complete Turf library open to the public is that at the Keeneland Race Course, Lexington, which includes approximately 3,000 volumes, fully catalogued.

Most famous racer of the century in America is MAN O' WAR, shown here shortly after he was retired from training at the end of the 1920 season. As points of conformation, the high withers and short cannons should be particularly noted, as well as the relation between height and length. Man o' War was an exceptional type of racer, having blinding speed at short distances plus the ability to stay at longer ones.

R. L. McClure.

LaVergne, TN USA
07 April 2010
178370LV00001B/150/A